" Flowers, penny a bunch."

Old London Street Cries

AND THE CRIES OF TO-DAY

WITH

Heaps of Quaint Cuts

BY

ANDREW W. TUER,
Author of " Bartolozzi and his Works," &c.

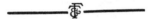

LONDON
The Scolar Press
1978

Reprinted in Great Britain by
The Scolar Press Ltd, Ilkley, Yorkshire,
from the edition of 1885 printed and published by
The Leadenhall Press, London, E.C.
ISBN 0 85967 402 9

Introductory.

~~~

THE "Cries"* have been sufficiently well received in bolder form at a guinea to induce the publication of this additionally illustrated extension at the more popular price of a shilling.

Old London Street Cries.

———◆———

DATES, unless in the form of the luscious fruit of Smyrna, are generally dry. It is enough therefore to state that the earliest mention of London Cries is found in a quaint old ballad entitled "London Lyckpenny," or Lack penny, by that prolific writer, John Lydgate, a Benedictine monk of Bury St. Edmunds, who flourished about the middle of the fifteenth century.

These cries are particularly quaint, and especially valuable as a record of the daily life of the time.

＊　＊　＊　＊　＊　＊　＊

Then unto London I dyd me hye,
  Of all the land it beareth the pryse :
Hot pescodes, one began to crye,
  Strabery rype, and cherryes in the ryse ; ＊

＊ On the bough.

"*I love a Ballad in print, a'life; for then we are sure they are true.*"—WINTER'S TALE, Act. iv., Sc. iii.

One bad me come nere and by some spyce,
   Peper and safforne they gan me bede,
   But for lack of money I myght not spede.

Then to the Chepe I began me drawne,
   Where mutch people I saw for to stande ;
One spred me velvet, sylke, and lawne,
   Another he taketh me by the hande,
" Here is Parys thred, the fynest in the land ; "
   I never was used to such thyngs indede,
   And wantyng money I myght not spede.

Then went I forth by London stone,
   Throughout all Canwyke * Streete ;
Drapers mutch cloth me offred anone,
   Then comes me one cryed hot shepes feete ;
One cryde makerell, ryster † grene, an other gan greete ;
   On bad me by a hood to cover my head,
   But for want of mony I myght not be sped.

Then I hyed me into Est-Chepe ;
One cryes rybbs of befe, and many a pye ;

*   *   *   *   *   *   *

   Since Lydgate's time the cries of London have been
a stock subject for ballads and children's books, of

---

   * Candlewick.   † Rushes green.

                         which

which, in various forms, some hundreds must have appeared within the last two centuries. The cuts, unless from the hand of a Rowlandson or a Cruikshank, are usually of the mechanical order; and one finds copies of the same illustrations, though differently treated, constantly reappearing.

In the books there is usually a cut on each page, with a cry printed above or underneath, and in addition a verse of descriptive poetry, which, if not of the highest order, serves its purpose.

> With his machine and ass to help
>   To draw the frame along,
> Pray mark the razor-grinder's yelp
>   The burden of his song.
> His patched umbrella quick aloft
>   He mounts if skies should lower,
> Then laughing whirls his wheel full oft,
>   Nor heeds the falling shower.

A well-known collection is that entitled " Habits & Cryes of the City of London, drawne after the Life; P. [Pearce] Tempest, excudit," containing seventy-four plates, drawn by Marcellus Laroon [Lauron], and republished in 1711. The first edition, with only fifty illustrations, had appeared some three-and-twenty years earlier; and many of the copper-plates in the
later

later issue were so altered as to bring the costume into the fashion of the time of republication. The hats had their high crowns cut down into low ; and shoe buckles were substituted for laces. Otherwise the plates,—with the exception of some of the faces, which were entirely re-engraved,—were left in their original condition.* The letter-press descriptions are in English, French, and Italian. The engraver, Marcellus Lauron, or Captain Laroon, who was born in London, has left on record that his family name was Lauron, but being always called Laroon, he adopted that spelling in early life. Of the seventy-four plates, those representing eccentric characters, etc., are omitted from the list that follows :—

Any Card Matches or Save Alls ?

Pretty Maids, Pretty Pins, Pretty Women !

" I remember," says Hone, " that pins were disposed of in this manner, in the streets by women. Their cry was a musical distich : —

> ' Three Rows a Penny pins,
> Short, Whites, and Mid-dl-ings !' "

Ripe Strawberryes !

---

* Mr. J. E. Gardner's collection of prints and drawings illustrating London, and numbering considerably over 120,000, contains many fine prints illustrating Old London Cries, including numerous examples of the alterations here indicated.

A

" Three Rows a Penny pins !"

A Bed Matt [mat] or a Door Matt !
Buy a fine Table Basket ?
Ha, ha, Poor Jack !

Can hardly be called a London cry: the call of a well-known character, who, accompanied by his wife, sold fish.

Buy my Dish of great Eeles ?

Buy

"Buy a fine Singing Bird?"

Buy a fine singing Bird?
Buy any wax or wafers?
Fine Writeing Ink!
A Right Merry Song!
Old Shooes for some Broomes!
Hott baked Wardens [stewed pears] Hott!
Small Coale!

Swift mentions this cry in his " Morning in Town."

" The Small Coal Man was heard with cadence deep
  Till drowned in shriller notes of 'Chimney Sweep.'"

Maids, any Coonie [rabbit] Skinns?
Buy a Rabbit, a Rabbit?
Chimney Sweep!
Crab, Crab, any Crab?
Oh, Rare Shoe!
Lilly White Vinegar!
Buy any Dutch Biskets?
Ripe Speregas! [asparagus]
Buy a Fork or a Fire Shovel? [See p. 13.]
Maids, buy a Mapp? [mop]
Buy my fat Chickens?
Buy my Flounders?
Old Cloaks, Suits, or Coats?

[Succeeding Old Doublets, the cry of a slightly earlier period.]

Fair Lemons and Oranges!

Old

"*Fine Writeing Ink!*"

Old Chaires to Mend ?
Twelve Pence a Peck, Oysters !
Troope every one ! [See p. 17.]

The man blowing a trumpet—troope every one !—was a
street seller of toy hobby-horses. He carried his wares in a
sort of cage ; and to each rudely represented horse's head was
attached a small flag. The toy hobby-horse has long since
disappeared, and nowadays we give a little boy a stick to thrust
between his legs as a Bucephalus. Hone opines that our forefathers were better natured, for they presented him with something of the semblance of the genuine animal.

Old Satten, Old Taffety, or Velvet !
Buy a new Almanack !
Buy my Singing Glasses !

These were long bell-mouthed glass tubes. The writer
recollects that when a boy he purchased, for a copper or two,
fragile glass trumpets of a similar description.

Any Kitchen Stuffe have you, Maids ?
Knives, Combs, or Inkhorns !
Four for Six Pence, Mackrell !
Any work for the Cooper ?
Four Paire for a Shilling, Holland Socks !
Colly Molly Puffe !

The cry of a noted seller of pastry. He is mentioned in
the *Spectator,* No. xxv.

Sixpence a pound, Fair Cherryes ! [See p. 21.]

Knives

"*Buy a Fork or a Fire Shovel?*"

Knives or Cisers to Grinde !
Long thread Laces, long and strong !
Remember the poor Prisoners !

In a series of early prints in the Bridgewater library, from copper plates, by an unknown artist, probably engraved between 1650 and 1680, there is one thus titled : " Some broken Breade and meate for ye poore prisoners : for the Lorde's sake pittey the poore." Within the memory of our fathers a tin box was put out from a grated window in the Fleet prison, a prisoner meanwhile imploring the public to remember the poor debtors. In the " Cries of York, for the amusement of young children," undated, but published probably towards the end of the last century, are the following lines :—

Of prisoners in the Castle drear
Come buy a Kalendar,
Their crimes and names are set down here
'Tis Truth I do declare.

A brass Pott or an Iron Pott to mend !
Buy my four ropes of Hard Onyons !
London's Gazette here !

The *London Gazette*, established in 1665.

Buy a White Line or a Jack Line, or a Cloathes Line.
Any old Iron take money for ?
Delicate Cowcumbers to pickle
Any Bakeing Peares ?
New River Water !

The

" Fine Oysters !"

The cry of "Marking Stones," which marked black or red, and preceded the daintier cedar-encased lead pencil of our own time, is not mentioned by Laroon. J. T. Smith,* says that the colour of the red marking-stone was due to "Ruddle," a colour not to be washed out, and that fifty years ago (he wrote in 1839) it was the custom at cheap lodging-houses to mark with it on linen the words, "*Stop thief!*"

The following lines are from a sheet of London Cries, twelve in number, undated, but probably of James the Second's time ;—

> Buy marking-stones, marking-stones buy,
> Much profit in their use doth lie ;
> I've marking-stones of colour red,
> Passing good, or else black lead.

In the British Museum is a folio volume containing another curious little collection, on three sheets, of early London cries ; also undated and of foreign

---

* "The Cries of London:" Copied from rare engravings or drawn from the life by John Thomas Smith, late Keeper of the Prints in the British Museum, 1839. On inquiring at the Print Department of the British Museum for a copy of this work, the attendant knew nothing of it, and was quite sure the department had no such book. It turned up on a little pressure, however, but the leaves were uncut.—*Les morts vont vite !*

workmanship,

"Troope every one!"

C

workmanship, but attributable to the time of Charles II. The first sheet has a principal representation of a rat-catcher with a banner emblazoned with rats ; he is attended by an assistant boy, and underneath are these lines :—

> He that will have neither
> Ratt nor mousse,
> Lett him pluck of the tilles
> And set fire of his hows.

Then come the following cries :

Cooper.
En of golde !
Olde Dublets !
Blackinge man.
Tinker.
Pippins !
Bui a matte !
Coales !
Chimney swepes.
Bui brumes !
Camphires ! [Samphire]
Cherrie ripe !
Alminake !
Coonie skine !
Mussels !

Cabeches !
Kitchen stuff !
Glasses !
Cockels !
Hartti Chaks !
Mackrill !
Oranges, Lemens !
Lettice !
Place !
Olde Iron !
Aqua vitæ !
Pens and Ink !
Olde bellows !
Herrings !
Bui any milke ?

Piepin

"Milk below, Maids!"

Piepin pys !	Turneps !
Osters !	Rossmarie Baie !
Shades !	Onions.

The principal figure on the second sheet is the "Belman," with halberd, lanthorn, and dog.

> Mayds in your Smocks, Loocke
> Wel to your locke—
> Your fire
> And your light,
> & God
> Give you good-night.
> At
> One o'Clock.

This is followed by :

Buy any shrimps ?	Good sasages !
Buy some figs ?	Buy a purs ?
Buy a tosting iron ?	Buy a dish a flounders ?
Lantorne Candellyht.	Buy a footestoole ?
Buy any maydes ?	Buy a fine bowpot ?
The Water Bearer.	Buy a pair a shoes ?
Buy a whyt pot ?	Buy any garters ?
Bread and Meate !	Featherbeds to dryue ?
Buy a candelsticke ?	Buy any bottens ?
Buy any prunes ?	Buy any whiting maps ?
Buy a washing ball ?	Buy any tape ?
	Worcestershyr

" Sixpence a pound,, Fair Cherryes!"

Worcestershyr salt !
Ripe damsons !
Buy any marking stoēs ?
The Bear bayting.
Buy any blew starch ?
Buy any points ?
New Hadog !

Yards and Ells !
Buy a fyne brush ?
Hote mutton poys !
New sprats new !
New cod new !
Buy any reasons ?
P. and glasses to mend !

The public "Cryer" on the third sheet, who
bears a staff and keys, humorously speaks as follows :

"O yis, any man or woman that
Can tell any tydings of a little
Mayden childe of the age of 24
Yeares.   Bring worde to the Cryer
And you shal be pleased for
Your labor,
And God's blessinge."

Then follow :

Buy any wheat ?
Buy al my smelts ?
Quick periwinckels !
Rype chesnuts !
Payres fyn !
White redish whyt !
Buy any whyting ?
Buy any bone lays ?

I ha rype straberies !
Buy a case for a hat ?
Birds and hens !
Hote podding pyes !
Buy a hair line ?
Buy any pompcons ?
Whyt scalions !
Rype walnuts !

Fine

" Songs, penny a sheet !"

Fyne potatos fyn !
Hote eele pyes !
Fresh cheese and creame?
Buy any garlick?
Buy a longe brush?
Whyt carots whyt !
Fyne pomgranats !
Buy any Russes?
Hats or caps to dress?
Wood to cleave?

Pins of the Maker !
Any sciruy gras?
Any cornes to pick?
Buy any parsnips?
Hot codlinges hot !
Buy all my soales?
Good morrow m.
Buy any cocumber?
New thornebacke !
Fyne oate cakes !

From all this it will be seen that merchandise of almost every description was formerly " carried and cried " in the streets. When shops were little more than open shanties, the apprentice's cry of " What d'ye lack, what d'ye lack my masters?" was often accompanied by a running description of the goods on sale, together with personal remarks, complimentary or otherwise, to likely and unlikely buyers.

A very puzzling London Cry, yet at one time a very common one, was "A tormentor for your fleas !" * What the instrument so heralded could have been, one can but dimly guess. A contributor to *Fraser's Magazine*, tells us that in a collection of London Cries appended to Thomas Heywood's *Rape of Lucrece*

---

* See Appendix.

(1608),

(1608), he gives us this one : " Buy a very fine mouse-trap, or a tormentor for your fleaes ;" and the cry of the mouse-trap man in Ben Jonson's Bartholomew Fair (1614), is, " Buy a mouse-trap, a mouse-trap, or a tormentor for a flea." The flea-trap is also alluded to in *The Bonduca* of Beaumont and Fletcher, and in *Travels of Twelve-Pence*, by Taylor, the Water Poet ; and it reappears in a broadside in the Roxburgh Collection of Ballads, " The Common Cries of London " [dated 1662, but probably written a hundred years earlier] : " Buy a trap, a mouse-trap, a torment for the fleas !" When the great Bard of the Lake School was on a tour, he made a call at an inn where Shelley happened to be ; but the conversation, which the young man would fain have turned to philosophy and poetry and art, was almost confined to the elder poet's prosaic description of his dog as " an excellent flea-trap." It may be assumed that fleas were plentiful when this cry was in vogue ; and it may have been that the trap was part of the (undressed ?) skin of an animal with the hair left on, in which fleas would naturally take refuge, drowning, perhaps, being their ultimate fate. But all this is mere conjecture.

It was unlikely that so close an observer of London life as Addison should leave unnoticed the Cries of London ; and the *Spectator* is interspersed with occasional

sional allusions to them. In No. ccli. we read: "There is nothing which more astonishes a Foreigner, and frights a Country Squire, than the Cries of London. My good Friend Sir ROGER often declares that he cannot get them out of His Head, or go to sleep for them, the first Week that he is in Town. On the contrary, WILL HONEYCOMB calls them the *Ramage de la Ville*, and prefers them to the Sounds of Larks and Nightingales, with all the Musick of the Fields and Woods."

In Steele's comedy of *The Funeral*, Trim tells some ragged soldiers, " There's a thousand things you might do to help out about this town, as to cry Puff-Puff Pyes ; have you any Knives or Scissors to grind ? or late in an evening, whip from *Grub Street* strange and bloody News from *Flanders ;* Votes from the House of Commons ; Buns, rare Buns ; Old Silver Lace, Cloaks, Sutes or Coats ; Old Shoes, Boots or Hats."

Gay, too, who, in his microscopic lyric of the streets, *Trivia*, omitted little, thus sings of various street cries :—

Now Industry awakes her busy sons ;
Full charged with News the breathless hawker runs ;
Shops open, coaches roll, carts shake the ground,
And all the streets with passing cries resound.

*　　*　　*　　*　　*　　*　　*

When

" Buy a Doll, Miss ?"

When all the Mall in leafy ruin lies,
And damsels first renew their Oyster cries.

* * * * * * *

When small coal murmurs in the hoarser throat,
From smutty dangers guard thy threatn'd coat.

* * * * * * *

What though the gathering mire thy feet besmear,
The voice of Industry is always near.
Hark ! the boy calls thee to his destined stand,
And the shoe shines beneath his oily hand.

Sadly he tells the tale of a poor Apple girl who lost
her life on the frozen Thames :—

Doll every day had walk'd these treacherous roads ;
Her neck grew warpt beneath autumnal loads
Of various fruit : she now a basket bore ;
That head, alas ! shall basket bear no more.
Each booth she frequent past, in quest of gain,
And boys with pleasure heard her shrilling strain.
Ah, Doll ! all mortals must resign their breath,
And industry itself submit to death !
The cracking crystal yields ; she sinks, she dies,
Her head chopt off from her lost shoulders flies ;
Pippins she cry'd ; but death her voice confounds ;
And *pip, pip, pip*, along the ice resounds.

Street cries have, before now, been made the vehicle
for

for Political Caricature, notably in *The Pedlars, or Scotch Merchants of London* (1763), attributed to the Marquis Townshend, which has particular reference to Lord Bute. Eliminating the political satire, we get a long list of street cries. The pedlars march two and two, carrying, of course, their wares with them. The vendors of food are numerous. One calls out " Dumplings, ho ! " another, who carries a large can, wishes to know " Who'l have a dip and a wallop for a bawbee ? " * Then come " Hogs Puddings ; " " Wall Fleet Oysters ; " " New Mackrel ; " " Sevil Oranges and Lemons ; " " Barcelona Philberts ; " " Spanish Chestnuts ; " " Ripe Turkey Figs ; " " Heart Cakes ; " " Fine Potatoes ; " " New-born Eggs, 8 a groat ; " " Bolognia Sausages." Miscellaneous wants are met with " Weather Cocks for little Scotch Courtiers ; " " Bonnets for to fit English heads ; " " Laces all a halfpenny a piece ; " " Ribbons a groat a yard ; " " Fine Pomatum ; " " Buy my Wash Balls, Gemmen and Ladies ; " " Fine Black Balls " (Blacking) ; " Buy a Flesh Brush ; " " Buy my Brooms ; " " Buy any Save-all or Oeconomy Pans, Ladies ; " " Water for the Buggs ; " * " Buy my pack-thread ; " " Hair or Combings " (for the manufacture of Wigs) ; " Any Kitchen Stuff ; " " Buy my Matches."

* See page 125.   Addison

Addison accuses the London street criers of culti-
vating the accomplishment of crying their wares so as
not to be understood ; and in that curious medley of
bons-mots and biographical sketches, " The Olio," by
Francis Grose,—dated 1796, but written probably
some twenty years earlier,—the author says, "The
variety of cries uttered by the retailers of different
articles in the streets of London make no inconsider-
able part in its novelty to strangers and foreigners.
An endeavour to guess at the goods they deal in
through the medium of language would be a vain attempt, as few of them convey any articulate sound. It
is by their tune and the time of day that the modern
cries of London are to be discriminated."

J. T. Smith says that the no longer heard cry of
" Holloway Cheese Cakes" was pronounced "*All my
Teeth Ache;*" and an old woman who sold mutton
dumplings in the neighbourhood of Gravel Lane called,
"*Hot Mutton Trumpery ;*" while a third crier, an old
man who dealt in brick-dust, used to shout something
that sounded exactly like "*Do you want a lick on the
head?*" Another man—a vendor of chickweed—brayed
like an ass ; while a stentorian bawler, who was described as a great nuisance, shouted "Cat's Meat,"
though he sold cabbages.

Indeed, some of the cries in our own day would
appear

appear to be just as difficult to distinguish. A lady tells me that in a poor district she regularly visits, the coal-cart man cries : " I'm on the woolsack ! " but what he means is, " Fine Wallsend Coal ! " The philologist will find the pronunciation of the peripatetic Cockney vendor of useful and amusing trifles—almost invariably penn'orths, by the way—worthy of careful study. Here are a couple of phonetically rendered examples : " Bettnooks, a penny fer two, two frer penny." [Button hooks, a penny for two, two for a penny.] " En endy shoo-awn frer penny." [A handy shoe-horn for a penny.]

Amongst the twelve etched London Cries " done from the life" by Paul Sandby, in 1766, and now scarce, are the following curious examples :—

My pretty little gimy [smart] tarter for a halfpenny stick, or a penny stick, or a stick to beat your Wives or Dust your cloths !

Memorandum books a penny a-piece of the poor blind. God bless you. Pity the blind !

Do you want any spoons — hard metal spoons ? Have you any old brass or pewter to sell or change ?

All fire and no smoke. A very good flint or a very good steel. Do you want a good flint or steel ?

Any tripe, or neat's foot or calf's-foot, or trotters, ho ! Hearts, Liver or Lights !

The

The simplers, or herb-gatherers, who were at one time numerous, supplied the herb-shops in Covent Garden, Fleet, and Newgate Markets. They culled from the hedges and brooks not only watercresses, of which London now annually consumes about £15,000 worth, but dandelions, scurvy grass, nettles, bitter-sweet, red valerian, cough-grass, feverfew, hedge mustard, and a variety of other simples. Notwithstanding the greater pungency of the wild variety, preferred on that account, of late years watercress-growing has been profitably followed as a branch of market gardening. In third-rate "genteel" neighbourhoods, where the family purse is seldom too well filled, "Creeses, young watercreeses," varied by shrimps or an occasional bloater, would appear to form the chief afternoon solace. Towards the end of the last century scurvy-grass was highly esteemed ; and the best scurvy-grass ale is said to have been sold in Covent Garden at the public-house at the corner of Henrietta Street.

The modern dealer in simples, who for a few pence supplies pills and potions of a more or less harmless character, calculated for the cure of every bodily ailment that afflicts humanity, flourishes in the poorer districts of London, and calls himself a herbalist. During the progress of an all too short acquaintance-
ship

ship struck up with a simpler in an Essex country lane through the medium of a particularly fragrant and soothing herb, the conversation happened on depression of spirits, and dandelion tea was declared to be an unfailing specific. " You know, sir, bad spirits means that the liver is out of order. The doctors gives you a deadly mineral pizen, which they calls blue pill, and it certainly do pizen 'em, but then you run the chance of being pizened yerself." A look of astonishment caused him to continue. " You've noticed the 'oles in a sheep's liver after it's cut up, 'aven't you ? Well, them 'oles is caused by slugs, and 'uman bein's is infested just the same. So is awsiz (horses), but they don't never take no blue pill. Catch 'em ! The doctors knows all about it, bless yer, but they don't talk so plain as me. *I* calls out-of-sort-ishness ' slugs in the liver,' and pizens 'em with three penn'rth of dandelion tea, for which I charges thrippence. *They* calls it ' sluggishness of the liver,' and pizens 'em with a penn'rth of blue pill, for which they charges a guinea, and as often as not they pizens the patient too." What a mine of " copy" that simple simpler would have proved to a James Payn or a Walter Besant !

The following at one time popular and often reprinted lines, to the tune of " The Merry Christ Church Bells," are from the Roxburgh Collection of Ballads :

D

Here's

Here's fine rosemary, sage and thyme.
Come buy my ground ivy.
Here's fetherfew, gilliflowers, and rue.
Come buy my knotted marjorum ho !
Come buy my mint, my fine green mint.
Here's lavender for your cloaths,
Here's parsley and winter savory,
And heartsease which all do choose.
Here's balm and hissop and cinquefoil,
All fine herbs, it is well known.
> Let none despise the merry, merry wives
> Of famous London town.

Here's pennyroyal and marygolds,
Come buy my nettle-tops.
Here's watercresses and scurvy grass.
Come buy my sage of virtue, ho !
Come buy my wormwood and mugwort.
Here's all fine herbs of every sort,
And southernwood that's very good,
Dandelion and horseleek.
Here's dragon's tongue and horehound.
> Let none despise the merry, merry wives
> Of famous London town.

Less characteristic is an old undated penny ballad from which we cull the following lines :—

Wood

Wood, three bundles a penny, all dried deal ;
Now, who'll buy a good flint or steel ?
Buy a walking stick, a good ash stump ;
Hearthstone, pretty maids, a penny a lump.
Fine mackrel ; penny a plateful sprats ;
Dog's meat, marm, to feed your cats.

The cry of Saloop, a favourite drink of the young bloods of a hundred and fifty years back, conveys no meaning to the present generation. Considered as a sovereign cure for drunkenness, and pleasant withal, saloop, first sold at street corners, where it was consumed principally about the hour of midnight, eventually found its way into the coffee houses. The ingredients used in the preparation of this beverage were of several kinds—sassafras, and plants of the genus known by the simplers as cuckoo-flowers, being the principal among them. Saloop finally disappeared some five and twenty years ago.

The watchman cried the time every half hour. In addition to a lantern and rattle, he was armed with a stout stick. T. L. Busby, who in 1819 illustrated " The Costumes of the Lower Orders of London," tells us that in March the watchman began his rounds at eight in the evening, and finished them at six in the morning. From April to September his hours were
from

from ten till five; and from November to the end of February, twelve till seven. During the darkest months there was an extra watch from six to twelve, and extra patrols or sergeants walked over the beats at intervals.

One of London's best known characters, the Waterman, does not appear to have adopted a cry; or, if he did, no mention of it can be found. But a correspondent of *Notes and Queries* (5th S. I. May 2, 1874) says: "I heard this verse of a very old (waterman's) song from a very old gentleman on the occasion of the last overflow of the Thames :—

"'Twopence to London Bridge, threepence to the Strand,
Fourpence, Sir, to Whitehall Stairs, or else you'll go by land.'"

The point of departure, however, is not given.

"Fine Tie or a fine Bob, Sir !" According to Hone, this was the cry in vogue at a time when everybody, old and young, wore wigs.* The price of a common one was a guinea, and every journeyman had a new

---

* "The best wigs are those made in Great Britain they beat the French and German ones all to sticks." *The Book of Aphorisms*, by a modern Pythagorean, 1834.

one

Rowlandson. Delin. 1819.

"Past one o'clock, an' a fine morning!"

one every year ; each apprentice's indenture stipulating, in the language of the officials who are still wig-wearers, that his master should find him in " one good and sufficient wig, yearly, and every year, for, and during, and unto, the expiration of the full end and term of his apprenticeship." A verse of the time tells us :—

Full many a year in Middle Row has this old barber been,
Which those who often that way go have full as often seen ;
Bucks, jemmies, coxcombs, bloods and beaux, the lawyer, the divine,
Each to this reverend tonsor goes to purchase wigs so fine.

" Buy my rumps and burrs ! " is a cry requiring a word of explanation. Before the skins of the newly flayed oxen were consigned to the tanner, the inside of the ear, called the burr, and the fleshy part of the tail were removed, and when seasoned and baked are said to have formed a cheap and appetising dish.

Ned Ward, the author of that curious work, " The London Spy " (1703), alludes to the melancholy ditty of " Hot baked Wardens [pears], and Pippins ; " and, in describing the amusements of Bartholomew Fair, states

states that in leaving a booth he was assailed with
" Will you buy a Mouse Trap or a Rat Trap? Will
you buy a Cloath Brush, or Hat Brush, or a Comb
Brush?" The writer possesses a very curious old
scenic aquatint print in the form of a fan mount,
representing Bartholomew Fair in 1721. The following descriptive matter is printed in the semicircular
space under the fan :—

" BARTHOLOMEW FAIR, 1721.

This fair was granted by Henry the 1st, to one
Rahere, a witty and pleasant gentleman of his Court,
in aid and for the support of an Hospital, Priory, and
Church, dedicated to St. Bartholomew, which he built
in repentance of his former profligacy and folly. The
succeeding Priors claimed, by certain Charters, to have
a Fair every year, during three days, viz. : on the Eve,
the Day, and on the Morrow of St. Bartholomew. At
this period the Clothiers of England, and drapers of
London, kept their Booths and Standings there, and a
Court of Piepouder was held daily for the settlement
of all Debts and Contracts. About the year 1721,
when the present interesting View of this popular Fair
was taken, the Drama was considered of some importance, and a series of minor although regular Pieces
were acted in its various Booths. At Lee and Harper's
the

the Siege of Berthulia is performing, in which is introduced the Tragedy of Holifernis. Persons of Rank
were also its occasional visitors, and the figure on the
right is supposed to be that of Sir Robert Walpole,
then Prime Minister. Fawkes, the famous conjuror,
forms a conspicuous feature, and is the only portrait
of him known to exist. The remaining amusements
are not unlike those of our day, except in the articles
of Hollands and Gin, with which the lower orders
were then accustomed to indulge, unfettered by licence
or excise."

Amongst the numerous figures represented on the
fan mount, but not mentioned by its publisher, Mr.
Setchel, is that of the crier of apples, whose basket is
piled high with tempting fruit. Another woman has
charge of a barrow laden with pears as big as pump-
kins ; and a couple of oyster-women, whose wares are
on the same gigantic scale, are evidently engaged in a
hot wrangle. Although foreign to our subject, it may
be mentioned that the statement as to the portrait of
Fawkes the conjuror being the only one known, is
incorrect.

Let not the ballad singer's shrilling strain
Amid the swarm thy listening ear detain :
Guard well thy pocket, for these syrens stand
To aid the labours of the diving hand ;

Confederate

"*Ye maidens and men, come for what you lack,
And buy the fair Ballads I have in my pack.*"
—Pedlar's Lamentation.

> Confederate in the cheat, they draw the throng,
> And Cambric handkerchiefs reward the song.

A state of things very graphically delineated in another print of " Barthelemew Fair " (1739), where a ballad singer is roaring out a *caveat against cut purses* whilst a pick-pocket is operating on one of his audience.

The old cry of " Marking Irons " has died out. The letters were cast in iron, and sets of initials were made up and securely fixed in long-handled iron boxes. The marking irons were heated and impressed as a proof of ownership.

> Hence ladders, bellows, tubs, and pails,
>   Brooms, benches, and what not,
> Just as the owner's taste prevails,
>   Have his initials got.

" My name and your name, your father's name and mother's name."

Hone says : " I well remember to have heard this cry when a boy. The type-seller composed my own name for me, which I was thereby enabled to imprint on paper with common writing ink. I think it has become wholly extinct within the last ten years."

Amongst later prints of the London Cries, none are at present so highly prized as the folio set engraved in
                                                          the

the early part of this century by Schiavonetti and others after Wheatley. Treated in the sentimentally pretty style of the period, they make, when framed, wall decorations which accord well with the prevailing old-fashioned furniture. If in good condition, the set of twelve will now readily fetch £20 at Christie's; and if coloured, £30 would not be considered too high a price, though five-and-twenty years ago they might easily have been picked up for as many shillings. Their titles are as follows :—

Knives, scissors, and razors to grind !
Old chairs to mend !
Milk below, maids !
Strawberrys, scarlet strawberrys !
Two bundles a penny, primroses, two bundles a penny !
Do you want any matches ?
Round and sound, fivepence a pound, Duke cherries !
Sweet China oranges !
Hot spiced gingerbread, smoking hot !
Fresh gathered peas, young Hastings !
A new love song, only a halfpenny apiece !
Turnips and carrots, oh !

In connection with the last cry, here is Dr. Johnson's humorous reference thereto :—

If

If the man who turnips cries,
Cry not when his father dies,
'Tis a proof that he had rather
Have a turnip than a father !

The modern bootblack with his " Clean yer boots,
shine 'em, sir ? " is the successor of the obsolete shoeblack, whose stock-in-trade consisted of liquid blacking, an old wig for removing dust or wet, a knife for
use on very muddy days, and brushes. Towards the
end of the last century, Finsbury Square—then an
open field—was a favourite place for shoeblacks, who
intercepted the city merchants and their clerks in their
daily walks to and from their residences in the villages
of Islington and Hoxton. At that time tight breeches
and shoes were worn ; and the shoeblack was careful
not to smear the buckles or soil the fine white stockings of his patrons. In a print of this period the cry
is " Japan your shoes, your honour ? " Cake blacking,
introduced by that famous, but, as regards the last
mentioned, somewhat antagonistic trio, Day, Martin,
and Warren, "the most poetical of blacking makers
and most transparent of poets," which was quickly
taken into general use, snuffed out the shoeblack ; and
from about 1820 until the time of the first Exhibition
in 1851, when the shoeblack brigade in connection
                                        with

" Fresh and sweet!"

with ragged schools was started, London may be said to have blacked its own boots.

"*Fresh Cabbidge!*"

Bill Sykes the coster-monger, or " costard "-monger, as he was originally called from his trade of selling apples, now flourishes under difficulties. What with the envious complaints of the small shopkeepers whom he undersells, and the supercilious rebuffs of the policeman who keeps him dodging about and always " on the move," Bill has a hard time of it indeed. Yet he is distinctly a benefactor to the poorer portion of humanity. He changes his cry with the stock on his barrow. He will invest one day in pine-apples, when there is a glut of them—perhaps a little over-ripe—in Pudding Lane ; and in stentorian voice will then make known his willingness to ex-change

change slices for a halfpenny each, or a whole one for sixpence. On other days it may be apples, or oranges, fish, vegetables, photographs, or even tortoises ; the latter being popularly supposed to earn a free, if un-comfortable, passage to this country in homeward-bound ships as wedges to keep the cargo from shifting in the hold. It is not often that goods intended for the thriving shopkeeper find their way to the barrow of the costermonger. Some time ago amber-tipped cherry or briar-wood pipes were freely offered and as freely bought in the streets at a penny each. Suddenly the supply stopped ; for the unfortunate wholesale dealer in Houndsditch, who might have known better, had mistaken " dozen " for " gross " in his advice ; and at 6s. 6d. per gross the pipes could readily be retailed for a penny each ; whereas at the cost price of 6s. 6d. a dozen, one shilling ought to have been asked. It seems that not only did the importer imagine that the amber mouthpieces were imitation, but Bill Sykes also thought he was "doing" the public when he announced them as real.

In the present race of street criers there are trick-sters in a small way ; as, for instance, the well known character who picks up a living by selling a bulky-looking volume of songs. His long-drawn and never varied cry of " Three un-derd an' fif-ty songs for a penny ! "

penny!" is really " Three under fifty songs for a penny." The book is purposely folded very loosely so as to bulk well ; but a little squeezing reduces it to the thickness of an ordinary tract. Street criers are honest enough, however, in the main. If vegetables are sometimes a little stale, or fruit is suspiciously over-ripe, they do not perhaps feel absolutely called upon to mention these facts ; but they give bouncing penn'-orths, and their clients are generally shrewd enough to take good care of themselves. Petty thieves of the area-sneak type use well-known cries as a blind while pursuing their real calling,—match-selling often serving as an opportunity for pilfering. Blacker sheep than these there are ; but fortunately one does not often come across them. Walking one foggy afternoon towards dusk along the Bayswater Road, I was accosted by a shivering and coatless vagabond who offered a tract. Wishing to shake off so unsavoury a companion, I attempted to cross the road, but a few yards from the kerb he barred further progress. " Sixpence, Sir, only sixpence, I *must* have sixpence!" and as he spoke he bared a huge arm knotted like a blacksmith's. Raising a fist to match, he more than once shot it out unpleasantly near, exhibiting every time he did so an eruption of biceps perfectly appalling in its magnitude. That tract is at home some-where. **There**

" *Antique Ballads, sung to crowds of old,*
 Now cheaply bought at thrice their weight in gold."

E

There are persons in London who get their living
by manufacturing amusing or useful penny articles,
with which they supply the wholesale houses in
Houndsditch, who in turn find their customers in the
hawkers and street criers. The principal supply, however, is imported from the Continent at prices against
which English labour cannot compete. Soon for-
gotten, each novelty has its day, and is cried in a
different manner. Until the law stepped in and put
a stop to the sale, the greatest favourite on public
holidays was the flexible metal tube containing scented
water, which was squirted into the faces of passers-by
with strict impartiality and sometimes with blinding
effect.

"All the fun of the fair,"—a wooden toy which,
when drawn smartly down the back or across the
shoulders, emits a sound as if the garment were being
rent—ranks, perhaps, second in the estimation of
'Arry and Emma Ann—she generally gets called
Emma Ran—when out for a holiday. "The Fun of
the Fair" is always about on public holidays, illumi-
nations, Lord Mayor's day, and in fact whenever
people are drawn out of doors in such multitudes that
the pathways are insufficient to hold the slowly moving
and densely packed human stream which perforce
slops over and amicably disputes possession of the
                                                    road

road with the confused and struggling mass of vehicles composed of everything that goes on wheels. A real Malacca cane, the smallest Bible in the world, a Punch and Judy squeaker, a bird warbler, a gold watch and chain, and Scotch bagpipes, are, with numerous others, at present popular and tempting penn'orths ; while the cry of " A penny for a shillin' 'lusterated magazine "—the epitaph on countless unsuccessful literary ventures—seems to many an irresistible attraction.

In connection with 'Arry, the chief producer of street noises, it may be questioned whether London is now much better off than it was before the passing of the Elizabethan Statutes of the Streets, by which citizens were forbidden, under pain of imprisonment, to blow a horn in the night, or to whistle after the hour of nine o'clock p.m. Sudden outcries in the still of the night, and the making of any affray, or the beating of one's wife—the noise rather than the brutality appears to have been objected to—were also specially forbidden. If this old Act is still on the Statute-book, it is none the less a dead letter. Our streets are now paraded by companies of boys or half-grown men who delight in punishing us by means of that blatant and horribly noisy instrument of dissonant, unchangeable chords, the German concertina.

In

In many neighbourhoods sleep is rendered, until the early hours, impossible by men and women who find their principal and unmolested amusement in the shouting of music-hall songs, with an intermittent accompaniment of shriekings. Professional street music of all kinds requires more stringent regulation ; and that produced by perambulating amateurs might with advantage be well-nigh prohibited altogether. The ringing of Church bells in the grey of the morning, and the early habits of the chanticleer, are often among the disadvantages of a closely populated neighbourhood. Nor are these street noises the only nuisances of the kind. London walls and partitions are nearly all thin, and a person whose neighbour's child is in the habit of practising scale exercises or "pieces," should clearly have the right to require the removal of the piano a foot or so from the wall, which would make all the difference between dull annoyance and distracting torment.

But we are wandering, and wandering into a dismal bye-way. Returning to our subject, it is impossible to be melancholy in the presence of the facetious salesman of the streets, with his unfailing native wit. Hone tells us of a mildly humorous character, one "Doctor Randal," an orange-seller, who varied the description of his fruit as circumstances and occasions

sions demanded; as "Oratorio oranges," and so on. A jovial rogue whose beat extends to numerous courts and alleys on either side of Fleet Street, regularly and unblushingly cries, "Stinking Shrimps," and by way of addenda, "Lor, 'ow they do stink to-day, to be sure!" His little joke is almost as much relished as his shrimps and bloaters, and they appear to be always of the freshest. Were it not that insufficient clothing and an empty stomach are hardly conducive thereto, the winter cry so generally heard after a fall of snow, "Sweep

"Stinking Fish!"

yer door away, mum?" might fairly be credited to an attempt at facetiousness under difficulties, while the grave earnestness of the mirth-provoking cry of the Cockney boot-lace man, "Lice, lice, penny a pair boot-lice!" is strong evidence that he has no
thought

thought beyond turning the largest possible number of honest pennies in the shortest possible space of time.

A search in our collection of books and ballads for London Cries, humorous in themselves, discovers but two,—

"Jaw-work, up and under jaw-work, a whole pot for a halfpenny, hazel-nuts!"

and—

"New laid eggs, eight a groat—crack 'em and try 'em!"

A somewhat ghastly form of facetiousness was a favourite one with a curious City character, now defunct. He was a Jew who sold a nameless toy—a dried pea loose in a pill box, which was fastened to a horse-hair, and on being violently twirled, emitted a vibratory hum that could be heard for some distance. Unless his unvarying cry, "On'y a 'a'penny," brought buyers to the fore, he gave vent to frequent explosions of strange and impious language, which never failed to provoke the merriment of the passer-by.

Among the many living City characters is the man —from his burr evidently a Northumbrian—who sells boot laces. His cry is, "Boot laces—AND the boot laces." This man also has a temper. If sales are

slow

" New laid eggs, eight a groat—crack 'em and try 'em!"

slow, as they not uncommonly are, his cry culminates
in a storm of muttered abuse ; after which mental
refreshment he calmly proceeds as before, " The boot
laces—AND the boot laces." Most of us know by
sight the penny Jack-in-the-box seller, whose cry, as
Jack pops up, on the spring of the lid being released,
is a peculiar double squeak, emitted without move-
ment of the lips. The cry is supposed to belong to
the internal economy of the toy, and to be a part of
the penn'orth ; but, alas ! Jack, once out of the hands
of his music-master, is voiceless. The numerous
street sellers of pipe and cigar lights must have a
hard time of it. Following the lucifer match, with its
attendant choking sulphurous fumes, came the evil-
smelling, thick, red-tipped, brown paper slip charged
with saltpetre, so that it should smoulder without
flaming. These slips, in shape something like a row
of papered pins, were divided half through and torn
off as required. Like the brimstone match which
preceded, and the Vesuvian which followed, these
lights (which were sold in the shops at a penny a box,
but in the streets at two and sometimes three boxes
for the same sum) utterly spoilt the flavour of a cigar ;
hence the superiority of the now dominant wax vestas.
The matches of a still earlier period were long slips
of dry wood smeared at either end with brimstone.
They

Rowlandson Delin 1819
"Letters for post?"

They would neither " light only on the box," nor off it, unless aided by the uncertain and always trouble-some flint, steel, and tinder, or the direct application of flame. " Clean yer pipe ; pipe-cleaner, a penny for two ! " is a cry seldom absent from the streets. The pipe-cleaner is a thin flexible, double-twisted wire about a foot long, with short bristles interwoven at one end, and now, " when everybody smokes who doesn't," the seller is sure of a more or less constant trade.

The buyers of the so-called penny ices sold in the London streets during the summer months are charged only a halfpenny ; and the numerous vendors, usually Italians, need no cry ; for the street *gamins* and errand boys buzz around their barrows like flies about a sugar barrel. For obvious reasons, spoons are not lent. The soft and half-frozen delicacy is consumed by the combined aid of tongue and fingers. Parti-coloured Neapolitan ices, vended by unmistakable natives of Whitechapel or the New Cut, whose curious cry of " 'Okey Pokey " originated no one knows how, have lately appeared in the streets. Hokey Pokey is of a firmer make and probably stiffer material than the penny ice of the Italians, which it rivals in public favour ; and it is built up of variously flavoured layers. Sold in halfpenny and also penny paper-covered
squares,

" Knives and Scissors to Grind ? "

squares, kept until wanted in a circular metal refriger-
ating pot surrounded by broken ice, Hokey Pokey has
the advantage over its rival eaten from glasses, inas-
much as it can be carried away by the purchaser
and consumed at leisure.   Besides being variously
flavoured, Hokey Pokey is dreadfully sweet, dreadfully cold, and hard as a brick.   It is whispered that
the not unwholesome Swede turnip, crushed into
pulp, has been known to form its base, in lieu of more
expensive supplies from the cow, whose complex
elaboration of cream from turnips is thus uncere-
moniously abridged.

Another summer cry recalls to memory a species of
house decoration, which we may hope is rapidly
becoming a thing of the past.   " Ornaments for yer
fire stoves," are usually either cream-tinted willow
shavings, brightened by the interspersion of a few
gold threads, or mats thickly covered with rose-shaped
bows and streamers of gaily-coloured tissue papers.
Something more ornate, and not always in better
taste, is now the fashion ; the trade therefore has
found its way from the streets to the shops, and the
old cry, " Ornaments for yer fire stoves," is likely to
be seldomer heard.

Many of the old cries, dying out elsewhere, may
still be familiar, however, in the back streets of second
                                                    and

"O' Clo!"

and third rate neighbourhoods. The noisy bell * of
the privileged muffin-man can
hardly be counted; but "dust, O,"
—the dustman's bell is almost a
thing of the past—"knives and
scissors," — pronounced sitthers
—"to grind," "chairs to mend,"
"cat's and dawg's meat," the
snapped-off short "o' clo" of the
Jewish dealer in left-off garments,
"fine warnuts, penny for ten, all
cracked," "chestnuts all 'ot," "fine
ripe strawberries," "rabbit or 'air
skins," "fine biggaroon cherries,'
"fine oranges, a penny for three,"
and many others, are still shouted
in due season by leathern-lunged
itinerant traders. The "O' clo"
man is nearly always historically
represented, as in the Catnach illustration, wearing

" Dust, O !"

---

* Francis Grose tells us, in 1796, that some trades have from
time immemorial invoked musical assistance,—such as those of
pie, post, and dust men, who ring a bell.

　　　　　My bell I keep ringing
　　　　　And walk about merrily singing
　　　　　My muffins.

　　　　　　　　　　　　　　　　several

Rowlandson. Delin. 1819.

" Cat's and Dog's Meat!"

several hats ; but, though he may often be met with more than one in his possession, he is now seldom seen with more than one on his head. Calling the price before the quantity, though quite a recent innovation, or more probably the revival of an old style, is almost universal. The cry of " Fine warnuts, ten a penny," is now " A penny for ten, fine warnuts," or " A penny for 'arf a score, fine warnuts."

The cat's meat man has never, like some of his colleagues, aspired to music, but apparently confines himself to the one strident monosyllable. It has been stated, by the way, that the London cats, of which it seems there are at present some 350,000, annually consume £100,000 worth of boiled horse. Daintily presented on a skewer, pussy's meat is eaten without salt ; but, being impossible of verification, the statistics presented in the preceding sentence may be taken with a grain.

" Soot" or " Sweep, ho ! " The sweep, accompanied by two or three thinly-clad, half-starved, and generally badly-treated apprentices, who ascended the chimneys and acted as human brushes, turned out in old times long before daylight. It was owing to the exertions of the philanthropist, Mr. Jonas Hanway, and before the invention of the jointed chimney sweeping machine, that an Act was passed at the beginning of this

ROYAL APP  OINTMENT

BY

F. W. EVANS

SHORT'S GARDENS—DRURY LANE

Famleys owning

Cats & Dogs

Waited on daily and regler.

NO CREDDIT

Fresh
Boiled
Paunfhes
once a
fortnite

Tripe
and
Taters
Cart
kept

this century, providing that every chimney-sweeper's apprentice should wear a brass plate in front of his cap, with the name and abode of his master engraved thereon. The boys were accustomed to beg for food and money in the streets ; but by means of the badges, the masters were traced, and an improvement in the general condition of the apprentices followed. But the early

" Sw-e-e-p !"

morning is still disturbed by the long-drawn cry, " Sw-e-e-p." This, and the not unmusical "ow-oo," of the jodeling milkman—all that is left of " milk below maids,"—the London milk-maids are usually strongly-built Irish or Welsh girls—and the tardier and rather too infrequent " dust-o " are amongst the few unsuppressed Cries of London-town. They are tolerated

" Ow-oo ! "

tolerated and continued because they are convenient, and from a vague sense of prescriptive right dear to the heart of an Englishman.

Until quite recently, the flower girls at the Royal Exchange—decent and well-behaved Irishwomen who work hard for an honest living—were badgered and driven about by the police. They are now allowed to collect and pursue their calling in peace by the Wellington statue, where their cry, "Buy a flower, sir," is heard, whatever the weather, all the year round. "Speshill 'dishun, 'orrible railway haccident," the outcome of an advanced civilization, is a cry that was unknown to our forefathers. Our forebears had often to pay a shilling for a newspaper, and the newsman made known his progress through the streets by sound of tin trumpet : as shown in Rowlandson's graphic illustration, a copy of the newspaper was carried in the hat-band.

Bertrand doong Delin. 1819.

"Great News!"

band. "C'gar lights, 'ere y'ar, sir; 'apenny a box," and "Taters all 'ot," also belong to the modern school of London Cries; while the piano-organ is a fresh infliction in connection with the new order of street noises. And although a sort of portable penthouse was used in remote times for screening from heat and rain, the ribbed and collapsible descendant thereof did not come into general use much before the opening of the present century; hence the cry, "Any umbrellas-termend," may properly be classed as a modern one.

In the crowded streets of modern London the loudest and most persistent cry is that of the omnibus conductor—"Benk," "Chairin' Krauss," "Pic'dilly"; or it may be, "Full inside," or "'Igher up"; to which the cabman's low-pitched and persuasive "Keb, sir?" —he is afraid to ply too openly for hire—plays an indifferent second. Judging from Rowlandson's illustration, his predecessor the hackney coachman shared cabby's sometimes too pointedly worded objection to a strictly legal fare.

The "under-street" Cries heard in our own time at the various stations on the railway enveloping London, in what by courtesy is termed a circle—the true shape would puzzle a mathematician to define—form an interesting study. While a good many of the porters are

Rowlandson Delin 1819.

"Wot d'yer call that?"

are recruited from the country, it is a curious fact that in calling the names of the various "sty-shuns" they mostly settle down—perhaps from force of association "downt-tcher-now"—into one dead level of Cockney pronunciation.

As one seldom realizes that there is anything wrong with one's own way of speaking, pure-bred Cockneys may be expected to quarrel with the phonetic rendering given ; however, as Dr. James Cantlie, in his interesting and recently published "Degeneration amongst Londoners," * tells us that a pure-bred Cockney is a *rara avis* indeed, the quarrelsomely inclined may not be numerous, and they may be reminded that the writer is not alone in his ideas as to Cockney pronunciation. Appended to Du Maurier's wonderfully powerful picture of "The Steam Launch in Venice" (Punch's Almanac, 1882), is the following wording :—

'Andsome 'Arriet : "Ow my ! if it 'yn't that bloomin' old Temple Bar, as they did aw'y with out o' Fleet Street !"

Mr Belleville (referring to Guide-book) : "No, it 'yn't ! It's the fymous Bridge o' SIGHS, as BYRON

---

* "Degeneration amongst Londoners." By James Cantlie, M.A., M.B., F.R.C.S. One Shilling. The Leadenhall Press, E.C.

went

went and stood on ; 'im as wrote OUR BOYS, yer
know ! "

'Andsome 'Arriet : " Well, I NEVER ! It 'yn't much
of a SIZE, any'ow ! "

Mr. Belleville : " ''Ear ! 'ear ! Fustryte ! "

This paragraph is from the London *Globe* of January
26th, 1885 : " Spelling reformers take notice. The English alphabet—diphthongs and all—does not contain
any letters which, singly or in combination, can convey
with accuracy the pronunciation given by the news-
boys to the cry, ' A-blowin' up of the 'Ouses of Parliament !' that rent the air on Saturday. The word
' blowin'' is pronounced as if the chief vowel sound
were something like ' ough ' in ' bough ' ; and even
then an ' e ' and a ' y ' ought to be got in some-
where."

There are twenty-seven stations on the London
Inner Circle Railway—owned by two companies, the
Metropolitan and District—and the name of one only
—Gower Street—is usually pronounced by " thet
tchung men," the railway porter, as other people pronounce it. [" Emma Smith,"* while not a main line
tation, may be cited here simply as a good example

---

* Hammersmith.

of Cockney, for 'Arry and 'Arriet are quite incapable of any other verbal rendering.] They are cried as follows :—

South Kenzint'nn."

" Glawster Rowd."
(owd as in " loud.")

" I Street, Kenzint'nn."

" Nottin' Ill Gite."
(ite as in " flight.")

" Queen's Rowd, Bize-water."
(ize as in " size.")

" Pride Street, Peddin-ten."

" Edge-wer Rowd."
(by common consent the Cockney refrains from saying " Hedge-wer.")

" Biker Street."

" Portland Rowd."

" Gower Street."

" King's Krauss."
(Often abbreviated to " 'ng's Krauss."

" Ferrinden Street."

" Oldersgit Street."
(no preliminary " H.")

" Mawgit Street."

" Bish-er-git."

" Ol'git."

" Mark Line."

" Monneym'nt."

" Kennun Street."

" Menshun Ouse."

" Bleckfriars."

" Tempull."
(" pull-pull-Tempull.")

" Chairin' Krauss."

" Wes'minster."
(One sometimes hears " Wes'-minister " : a provincialism.)

" S'n' Jimes-iz Pawk."
(ime as in " time.")

" Victaw-ia."

" Slown Square."
(own as in " town.")

Country cousins may be reminded that the guiding

guiding letters **I** or **O** so boldly marked on the tickets issued on the London underground railway, and, in the brightest vermilion, as conspicuously painted up in the various stations, do not mean "Inner" or "Outer" Circle, but the inner and outer lines of rails of the Inner Circle Railway. Though sanctioned by Parliament more than twenty years ago, the so-called Outer Circle Railway is still incom-

plete, its present form being that of a horse-shoe, with termini at Broad Street and Mansion House, and some of its principal stations at Dalston, Willesden, and Addison Road, Kensington.

It has before been said that everything that could be carried has, at some time or other, been sold in the streets ; and it follows that an approximately complete list of London Cries would reach a very large total. From its mere length and sameness such a list would moreover be apt to weary the reader ; for not all cries have the interest of a traditional phrase or intonation which gives notice of the nature of of the wares, even when the words are rendered unintelligible by the necessity of vociferation. But a few of the most constant and curious cries may be interesting to note.

"Hot Spice Gingerbread!"

"'Tis all hot, nice ſmoaking hot!"
    You'll hear his daily cry;
But if you won't believe, you ſot,
    You need but taste and try.

" Old

" *Old Cloaths!* "

Coats or preeches do you vant?
Or puckles for your ſhoes?
Vatches too me can ſupply :—
Me monies von't refuſe.

" *Knives*

"*Knives to Grind!*"

Young gentlemen attend my cry,
  And bring forth all your Knives;
The barbers Razors too I grind;
  Bring out your Sciffars, wives.

" *Cabbages*

" Cabbages O! Turnips!"

With mutton we nice turnips eat;
  Beef and carrots never cloy;
Cabbage comes up with Summer meat,
  With winter nice favoy.

Holloway

Holloway cheese cakes !
Large silver eels, a groat a pound, live eels !
Any New River water, water here ?
Buy a rope of onions, oh ?

" Sand 'O !"

Buy a goose ?
Any bellows to mend ?
Who's for a mutton pie, or an eel pie ?
Who buys my roasting jacks ?
Sand, ho ! buy my nice white sand, ho !

Buy

G "*Buy a Live Goose ?*"

Buy my firestone?
Roasted pippins, piping hot!

"Cherries, O! ripe cherries, O!"

A whole market hand for a halfpenny—young radishes, ho!
Sw-e-e-p!

Brick

"Fine Strawberries!"

Brick dust, to-day?
Door mats, want?
Hot rolls!
Rhubarb!
Buy any clove-water?
Buy a horn-book?
Quick (*living*) periwinkles!
Sheep's trotters, hot!
Songs, three yards a penny!
Southernwood that's very good!
Cherries O! ripe cherries O!
Cat's and dog's meat!
Samphire!
All a-growin', all a-blowin'.
Lilly white mussels, penny a quart!
New Yorkshire muffins!
Oysters, twelvepence a peck!
Rue, sage, and mint, farthing a bunch!
Tuppence a hundred, cockles!
Sweet violets, a penny a bunch!
Brave Windsor beans!
Buy my mops, my good wool mops!
Buy a linnet or a goldfinch?
Knives, combs, and inkhornes!
Six bunches a penny, sweet lavender!
New-laid eggs, eight a groat!

Any

" Sweet Lavender !"

Any wood?

Hot peas!

Hot cross buns!

Buy a broom?

Old chairs to mend!

Young lambs to sell!

Tiddy diddy doll!

Hearth-stone!

Buy my nice drops, twenty a penny, peppermint drops!

Any earthen ware, plates, dishes, or jugs, to-day,—any clothes to exchange, Madam?

Holly O, Mistletoe!

Buy my windmills for a ha'penny a piece! [a child's toy.]

Nice Yorkshire cakes!

Buy my matches, maids, my nice small pointed matches!

Come, buy my fine myrtles and roses!

Buy a mop or a broom?

Hot rolls!

Will you buy a Beau-pot?

Probably of Norman-French origin, the term " beau-pot" is still in use in out-of-the-way country districts, to signify a posy or nosegay, in which sweet-smelling herbs and flowers, as rosemary, sweet-briar, balm,

roses,

"Chairs to mend!"

roses, carnations, violets, wall-flowers, mignonette,
sweet-William, and others that we are now pleased to

" All a blowin' !"

designate "old fashioned," would naturally predomi-
nate.

Come buy my sweet-briar !

Any

Rowlandson Delin 1819.

"Any Earthen Ware; buy a jug or a tea pot?"

Any old flint glass or broken bottles for a poor woman to-day

"Fresh Oysters! penny a lot!"

Sweet primroses, four bunches a penny, primroses !
Black and white heart cherries, twopence a pound,
full weight, all round and sound !

Fine

"Buy my Sweet Roses?"

Fine ripe duke cherries, a ha'penny a stick and a penny a stick, ripe duke cherries !

Shrimps like prawns, a ha'penny a pot !

Green hastings !

"Fine large Cucumbers !"

Hot pudding !

Pots and kettles to mend !

'Ere's yer toys for girls an' boys !

Brick-dust was carried on the backs of asses and sold for knife-cleaning purposes at a penny a quart.

The

"'Ere's yer toys for girls an' boys!"

The bellows-mender, who sometimes also followed the trade of a tinker, carried his tools and apparatus buckled in a leathern bag at his back, and practised his profession in any convenient corner of the street.

Door-mats of all shapes were made of rushes or rope, and were sold at from sixpence to several shillings each.

The earliest green pea brought to the London market—a dwarf variety—was distinguished by the name of Hasteds, Hastens, Hastins, or Hastings, and was succeeded by the Hotspur. The name of Hastings was, however, indiscriminately given to all peas sold in the streets, and the cry of "green Hastings" was heard in every street and alley until peas went out of season.

The crier of hair brooms, who usually travelled with a cart, carried a supply of brushes, sieves, clothes-horses, lines, and general turnery.

> All cleanly folk must like my ware,
> For wood is sweet and clean ;
> Time was when platters served Lord Mayor
> And, as I've heard, a Queen.

His cry took the form of the traditional tune " Buy a broom," which may even now be occasionally heard —perhaps the last survival of a street-trade tune—

taken

Rowlandson, Delin. 1819.

Curds and Whey!

taken up separately or in fitful chorus by the men and women of a travelling store. The Flemish "Buy a Broom" criers, whose trade is gone, generally went in couples or threes. Their figures are described by Hone as exactly miniatured in the unpainted wooden doll, shaped the same before and behind, and sold in the toy shops for the amusement of the little ones. In the comedy of "The Three Ladies of London," printed in quarto in Queen Elizabeth's reign (A.D. 1584), is this passage :—

"Enter Conscience with brooms at her back, singing as follows :—

New brooms, green brooms, will you buy any?
Maydens come quickly, let me take a penny."

Hot rolls, which were sold at one and two a penny, were carried during the summer months between the hours of 8 and 9 in the morning, and from 4 to 6 in the afternoon.

Let Fame puff her trumpet, for muffin and crumpet,
    They cannot compare with my dainty hot rolls ;
When mornings are chilly, sweet Fanny, young Billy,
    Your hearts they will comfort, my gay little souls.

Muffins and crumpets were then, as now, principally cried during the winter months.

Hot

Hot pudding, sweet, heavy and indigestible, was sold in halfpenny slabs.

> Who wants some pudding nice and hot!
> 'Tis now the time to try it;
> Just taken from the smoking pot,
> And taste before you buy it.

The cry "One-a-penny, two-a-penny, *hot* CROSS BUNS!" which,—now never heard from the sellers on Good Friday,—is still part of a child's game, remains as one of the best instances of English quantitative metre, being repeated in measured time, and not merely by the ordinary accent. The rhubarb-selling Turk, who appeared in turban, trousers, and —what was then almost unknown amongst civilians —moustaches, was, fifty years ago or more, a well-known character in the metropolis.

Sand was generally used in London, not only for cleaning kitchen utensils, but for sprinkling over uncarpeted floors as a protection against dirty footsteps. It was sold by measure—red sand, twopence halfpenny, and white a penny farthing per peck. The very melodious catch, "White Sand and Grey Sand, Who'll buy my White] Sand!" was evidently harmonized on the sand-seller's traditional tune.

"Buy a bill of the play!" In the time of our great
H   grandfathers,

grandfathers, there were no scented programmes, and the peculiar odour of the play-bills was not due to the skill of a Rimmel. Vilely printed with the stickiest of ink, on the commonest of paper, they were disposed of both in and outside the theatre by orange-women, who would give one to a purchaser of half a dozen oranges or so. In Hogarth's inimitably amusing and characteristic print of *The Laughing Audience,* a couple of robustly built orange-women are contending, with well-filled baskets, for the favour of a bewigged beau of the period, who appears likely to become an easy victim to their persuasions.

" Knives to Grind " is still occasionally heard, and the grinder's barrow (*vide* that depicted in Rowland-son's illustration on p. 59), is much the same as it was a hundred years ago. At the beginning of the century the charge for grinding and setting scissors was a penny or twopence a pair ; penknives a penny a blade, and table-knives one and sixpence and two shillings a dozen.

Rabbits were carried about the streets suspended at either end of a pole which rested on the shoulder.

The edible marine herb samphire, immortalized in connection with " Shakespeare's Cliff" at Dover, was at one time regularly culled and as regularly eaten.

The once familiar cry of " Green rushes O ! " is preserved

" Cherries, fourpence a pound !"

served only in verse. In Queen Elizabeth's time the floors of churches as well as private houses were carpeted with rushes, and in Shakespeare's day the stage was strewn with them. Rush-bearing, a festival having its origin in connection with the annual renewal of rushes in churches, was kept up until quite recently, and may even still be practised in out-of-the way villages.

The stock of the " 'arthstone" woman, who is not above doing a stroke of business in bones, bottles, and kitchen stuff, is usually on a barrow, drawn by a meek-eyed and habitually slow-paced donkey.

The London Barrow Woman (" Ripe Cherries"), as preserved in the cut from the inimitable pencil of George Cruikshank, has long since disappeared. In 1830, when this sketch was made, the artist had to rely on his memory, for she then no longer plied her trade in the streets. Her wares changed with the seasons ; but here a small schoolboy is being tempted by ripe cherries tied on a stick. There being no importation of foreign fruit, the cherries were of prime quality. May dukes, White heart, Black heart, and the Kentish cherry, succeeded each other—and, when sold by weight, and not tied on sticks, fetched sixpence, fourpence, or threepence per lb., which was at least twopence or threepence less than charged at the shops.

The

"Ripe Cherries!"

The poor Barrow Woman appears to have been treated very much in the same manner as the modern coster-monger; but was without his bulldog power of re-sistance. If she stopped to rest or solicit custom, street keepers, "authorized by orders unauthorized by law," drove her off, or beadles overthrew her fruit into the road. Nevertheless, if Cruikshank has not idealized his memories, she was more wholesomely and stoutly clad than any street seller of her sex—with the one exception of the milkmaid—who is to be seen in our day, when the poor London woman has lost the instinct of neatness and finish in attire.

"Hot spiced gingerbread," still to be found in a cold state at village fairs and junketings, used to be sold in winter time in the form of flat oblong cakes at a halfpenny each, but it has long since disappeared from our streets.

"Tiddy Diddy Doll, lol, lol, lol" was a celebrated vendor of gingerbread, and, according to Hone, was always hailed as the king of itinerant tradesmen. It must be more than a century since this dandified character ceased to amuse the populace. He dressed as a person of rank—ruffled shirt, white silk stockings, and fashionable laced suit of clothes surmounted by a wig and cocked hat decorated with a feather. He was sure to be found plying his trade on Lord Mayor's day

"Tiddy Diddy Doll."

day, at open-air shows, and on all public occasions. He amused the crowd to his own profit; and some of his humorous nonsense has been preserved.

"Mary, Mary, where are you *now*, Mary?"

"I live two steps underground, with a wiscom riscom, and why not. Walk in, ladies and gentlemen. My shop is on the second floor backwards, with a brass knocker at the door. Here's your nice gingerbread, your spiced gingerbread, which will melt in your mouth like a red-hot brickbat, and rumble in your inside like Punch in his wheelbarrow!" He always finished up by singing the fag end of a song— "Tiddy Diddy Doll, lol, lol, lol;" hence his nickname of Tiddy Doll. Hogarth has introduced this character in his Execution scene of the Idle Apprentice at Tyburn. Tiddy Doll had many feeble imitators; and the woman described in the lines that follow, taken from a child's book of the period, must have been one of them.

> Tiddy Diddy Doll, lol, lol, lol,
> Tiddy Diddy Doll, dumplings, oh!
> Her tub she carries on her head,
> Tho' of'ener under arm.
> In merry song she cries her trade,
> Her customers to charm.

A

A halfpenny a plain can buy,
The plum ones cost a penny,
And all the naughty boys will cry
Because they can't get any.

" Large silver eels !"

Fifty years ago "Young Lambs to Sell, two for a penny," which still lingers, was a well known cry. They were children's toys, the fleece made of white cotton-wool, attractively but perhaps a trifle too unnaturally

naturally spangled with Dutch gilt. The head was of composition, the cheeks were painted red, there were two black spots to do duty for eyes, and the horns and legs were of tin, which latter adornment, my younger readers may suggest, foreshadowed the insufficiently appreciated tinned mutton of a later period. The addition of a bit of pink tape tied round the neck by way of a collar made a graceful finish, and might be accepted as a proof that the baby sheep was perfectly tame.

> Young lambs to sell, young lambs to sell.
> Two for a penny, young lambs to sell.
> If I'd as much money as I could tell,
> I wouldn't cry young lambs to sell.
> Dolly and Molly, Richard and Nell,
> Buy my Young Lambs and I'll use you well !

The later song—

> Old chairs to mend, old chairs to mend.
> If I'd as much money as I could spend,
> I'd leave off crying old chairs to mend—

—is obviously copied from the original cry of " Young Lambs to Sell." In addition to a few tools, the stock-in-trade of the travelling chair-mender principally consisted of rushes which in later days gave place to cane split into strips of uniform width—a return to more ancient

Young lambs to sell."

ancient practice. The use of rush-bottomed chairs, which are again coming into æsthetic fashion, cannot

" Buy my fine Myrtles and Roses ! "

be traced back quite a century and a half. The chairs in Queen Anne's time were seated and backed with cane ; and in the days of Elizabeth the seats were cushioned

cushioned and the backs stuffed. Many years ago an
old chair-mender occupied a position by a stone fixed
in the wall of one of the houses in Panyer Alley, on
which is cut the following inscription :—

WHEN Y HAVE SOVGHT:
THE CITY ROVND
YET STILL THIS IS
THE HIGHST: GROVND
AVGVST THE 27

1688

Being

Being entirely unprotected and close to the ground, this curious relic of bygone times, which is surmounted by a boldly carved figure of a nude boy seated on a panyer pressing a bunch of grapes between his hand and foot, is naturally much defaced ; and that it has not been carried away piecemeal by iconoclastic curiosity-hunters, is probably due to its out-of-the-way position.   Panyer Alley, the most eastern turning leading from Paternoster Row to Newgate Street, slightly rises towards the middle ; but is not, according to Mr. Loftie, an undoubted authority on all matters pertaining to old London, the highest point in the city, there being higher ground both in Cornhill and Cannon Street.   In describing Panyer Alley, Stow indirectly alludes to a " signe " therein, and it is Hone's opinion that this stone may have been the ancient sign let into the wall of a tavern.   While the upper is in fair preservation, the lower part of the inscription can hardly be read.   When last examined, a street urchin was renovating the figure by a heartily-laid-on surface decoration of white chalk ; and unless one of the numerous antiquarian or other learned societies interested in old London relics will spare a few pounds for the purchase of a protective grating, there will shortly be nothing left worth preserving.

" New-laid eggs, eight a groat," takes us back to a time

time when the best joints and fresh country butter
were both sixpence a pound.

Years ago the tin oven of the peripatetic penny pieman was found to be too small to meet the constant
and ever-increasing strain made upon its resources ;
and the owner thereof has now risen to the dignity of
a shop, where, in addition to stewed eels, he dispenses
what Albert Smith happily termed "covered uncertain-
ties," containing messes of mutton, beef, or seasonable
fruit.　Contained in a strong wicker basket with legs,
or in a sort of tin oven, the pieman's wares were formerly kept hot by means of a small charcoal fire.　A
sip of a warm stomachic liquid of unknown but apparently acceptable constituents was sometimes offered
gratuitously by way of inducement to purchase.　The
cry of "Hot Pies" still accompanies one of the first
and most elementary games of the modern baby learn-
ing to speak, who is taught by his nurse to raise his
hand to imitate a call now never heard.

The specimens of versification that follow are
culled from various books of London Cries, written
for the amusement of children, towards the end of the
last century, and now in the collection of the writer :—

Large silver eels—a groat a pound, live eels !
　　　Not the Severn's famed stream
　　　　Could produce better fish,

　　　　　　　　　　　　Sweet

Sweet and fresh as new cream,
    And what more could you wish?

Pots and Kettles to mend?

Your coppers, kettles, pots, and stew pans,
Tho' old, shall serve instead of new pans.
I'm very moderate in my charge,
For mending small as well as large.

Buy a Mop or a Broom!

My mop is so big, it might serve as a wig
    For a judge if he had no objection,
And as to my brooms, they'll sweep dirty rooms,
    And make the dust fly to perfection.

Nice Yorkshire Cakes!

Nice Yorkshire cakes, come buy of me,
    I have them crisp and brown;
They are very good to eat with tea,
    And fit for lord or clown.

Buy my fine Myrtles and Roses!

Come buy my fine roses, my myrtles and stocks,
My sweet-smelling balsams and close-growing box.

Buy my nice Drops—twenty a penny, Peppermint
drops!

If

Rowlandson N. Delin. 1810

I   "*Pots and Kettles to Mend!*"

If money is plenty you may sure spare a penny,
It will purchase you twenty—and that's a great many.

Six bunches a penny, sweet blooming Lavender!

> Just put one bundle to your nose,
>   What rose can this excel?
> Throw it among your finest clothes,
>   And grateful they will smell.

Buy a live Chicken or a young Fowl?

> Buy a young Chicken fat and plump,
>   Or take two for a shilling?—
> Is this poor honest tradesman's cry;
>   Come buy if you are willing.

Rabbit! Rabbit!

> Rabbit! a Rabbit! who will buy?
>   Is all you hear from him;
> The rabbit you may roast or fry,
>   The fur your cloak will trim.

My good Sir, will you buy a Bowl?

> My honest friend, will you buy a Bowl,
>   A Skimmer or a Platter?
> Come buy of me a Rolling Pin
>   Or Spoon to beat your batter.

Come

" Six bunches a penny, sweet blooming Lavender ! "

Come buy my fine Writing Ink !

    Through many a street and many a town
      The Ink-man shapes his way :
    The trusty Ass keeps plodding on,
      His master to obey.

Dainty Sweet-Briar !

    Sweet-Briar this Girl on one side holds,
      And Flowers in the other basket ;
    And for the price, she that unfolds
      To any one who'll ask it.

Any Earthen Ware, Plates, Dishes, or Jugs to-day,—
any Clothes to exchange, Madam ?

    Come buy my Earthen Ware
      Your dresser to bedeck ;
    Examine it with care,
      There's not a single speck.

    See white with edges brown,
      Others with edges blue ;
    Have you a left-off gown,
      Old bonnet, hat, or shoe ?

    Do look me up some clothes
      For this fine China jar ;

                        If

If but a pair of shoes,
    For I have travelled far.

This flowered bowl of green
    Is worth a gown at least ;
I am sure it might be seen
    At any christening feast.

Do, Madam, look about
    And see what you can find ;
Whatever you bring out
    I will not be behind.

The Illustrations.

Ten of the illustrations by that great master of the art of caricature, Thomas Rowlandson, are copied in *facsimile* from a scarce set, fifty-four in all, published in 1820, entitled "Characteristic Sketches of the Lower Orders," to which there is a powerful preface, as follows :—

"The British public must be already acquainted with numerous productions from the inimitable pencil of MR. ROWLANDSON, who has particularly distinguished himself in this department.

"There is so much truth and genuine feeling in his
                           delineations

delineations of human character, that no one can inspect the present collection without admiring his masterly style of drawing and admitting his just claim to originality. The great variety of countenance, expression, and situation, evince an active and lively feeling, which he has so happily infused into the drawings as to divest them of that broad caricature which is too conspicuous in the works of those artists who have followed his manner. Indeed, we may venture to assert that, since the time of Hogarth, no artist has appeared in this country who could be considered his superior or even his equal."

The two illustrations—"Lavender," with a background representing Temple Bar, and "Fine Strawberries," with a view of Covent Garden—are from "Plates Representing the Itinerant Traders of London in their ordinary Costume. Printed in 1805 as a supplement to 'Modern London' (London : printed for Charles Phillips, 71, St. Paul's Churchyard)." The set is chiefly interesting as representing London scenes of the period ; many parts of which are now no longer recognisable.

The crudely drawn, but picturesquely treated "Catnach" cuts, from the celebrated Catnach press in Seven Dials, now owned by Mr. W. S. Fortey, hardly require separately indicating.

The

The four oval cuts, squared by the addition of per-
pendicular lines, " Hot spice gingerbread ! " " O' Clo ! "
" Knives to Grind ! " and " Cabbages O ! Turnips ! "
are facsimiled from a little twopenny book, entitled,
" The Moving Market ; or, Cries of London, for the
amusement of good children," published in 1815 by
J. Lumsden and Son, of Glasgow. It has a frontispiece representing a curious little four-in-hand carriage
with dogs in place of horses, underneath which is
printed this triplet :—

> See, girls and boys who learning prize,
> Round London drive to hear the cries,
> Then learn your Book and ride likewise.

The quaint cuts, " Ere's yer toys for girls an' boys ! "
" New-laid eggs, eight a groat,—crack 'em and try
'em ! " " Flowers, penny a bunch ! " (frontispiece), and
the three ballad singers, apparently taken from one of
the earliest chap-books, are really but of yesterday.
For these the writer is indebted to his friend, Mr.
Joseph Crawhall, of Newcastle-on-Tyne, who uses his
cutting tools direct on the wood without any copy. Mr.
Crawhall's " Chap-book Chaplets," and " Olde ffrendes
wyth newe Faces," quaint quartos each with many
hundreds of hand-coloured cuts in his own peculiar
and inimitable style, and " Izaak Walton, his Wallet
Booke," are fair examples of his skill in this direction.

Two

Two plates unenclosed with borders—"Old Chairs to mend!" and "Buy a Live Goose?" are from that once common and now excessively scarce child's book, *The Cries of London as they are Daily Practised*, published in 1804 by J. Harris, the successor of "honest John Newbery," the well-known St. Paul's Churchyard bookseller and publisher.

George Cruikshank's London Barrow-woman ("Ripe Cherries"), "Tiddy Diddy Doll," and other cuts, are from the original illustrations to Hone's delightful "Every-Day Book," recently republished by Messrs. Ward, Lock & Co.

The cuts illustrating modern cries—"Sw-e-e-p!"; "Dust, O!"; "Ow-oo!"; "Fresh Cabbidge!"; and "Stinking Fish!" are from the facile pencil of Mr. D. McEgan.

Finally, in regard to the business card of pussy's butcher, the veracious chronicler is inclined to think that an antiquarian might hesitate in pronouncing it to be quite so genuine as it looks. This opinion coincides with his own. In fact he made it himself. As a set-off, however, to the confession, let it be said that this is the sole *fantaisie d'occasion* set down herein.

——o——

APPENDIX

APPENDIX.

From "Notes and Queries."

LONDON STREET CRY.—What is the meaning of the old London cry, " Buy a fine mousetrap, or a *tormentor for your fleas* "?   Mention of it is found in one of the Roxburghe ballads dated 1662, and, amongst others, in a work dated about fifty years earlier.   The cry torments me, and only its elucidation will bring ease.

ANDREW W. TUER.

The Leadenhall Press, E.C.

LONDON STREET CRY (6th S. viii. 348).—Was not this really a " tormentor for your *flies* " ?   The mousetrap man would probably also sell little bunches of butcher's broom (*Ruscus*, the mouse-thorn of the Germans), a very effective and destructive weapon in the hands of an active butcher's boy, when employed to guard his master's meat from the attacks of flies.

EDWARD SOLLY.

LONDON

LONDON STREET CRY (6th S. viii. 348, 393).—The following quotations from Taylor, the Water Poet, may be of interest to Mr. TUER :—

> "I could name more, if so my Muse did please,
>   Of Mowse Traps, and tormentors to kill Fleas."
>   *The Travels of Twelve-pence.*

> "Yet shall my begg'ry no strange Suites devise,
>   As monopolies to catch Fleas and Flyes."
>   *The Beggar.*

Faringdon.   WALTER HAINES.

I notice a query from you in *N. and Q.* about a London Street Cry which troubles you. Many of the curious adjuncts to Street Cries proper have, I apprehend, originally no meaning beyond drawing attention to the Crier by their whimsicality. I will give you an instance. Soon after the union between England and Ireland, a man with a sack on his back went regularly about the larger streets of Dublin. His cry was :

> "Bits of Brass,
>   Broken Glass,
>   Old Iron,
>   Bad luck to you Castlereagh."

Party

Party feeling against Lord Castlereagh ran very high at the time, I believe, and the political adjunct to his cry probably brought the man more shillings than he got by his regular calling.

H. G. W.

P.S.—I find I have unconsciously made a low pun. The cry alluded to above would probably be understood and appreciated in the streets of Dublin at the present with reference to the Repeal of the Union.

LONDON STREET CRY.

88, FRIARGATE, DERBY.

DEAR SIR,–

The "Tormentor," concerning which you inquire in *Notes and Queries* of this date, was also known as a "Scratch-back," and specimens are occasionally to be seen in the country. I recollect seeing one, of superior make, many years ago. An ivory hand, the fingers like those of "Jasper Packlemerton of atrocious memory," were "curled as in the act of" scratching, a finely carved wrist-band of lace was the appropriate ornament, and the whole was attached to a slender ivory rod of say eighteen inches in length. The finger nails were sharpened, and the instrument was thus available for discomfiting "back-biters," even when
engaged

engaged upon the most inaccessible portions of the human superficies. I have also seen a less costly article of the same sort carved out of pear-wood (or some similar material). It is probable that museums might furnish examples of the " back scratcher," " scratch back," or " tormentor for your fleas."

Very truly yours,
ALFRED WALLIS.

JUNIOR ATHENÆUM CLUB,
PICCADILLY, W.

DEAR SIR,—

On turning over the leaves of *Notes and Queries*, I happened on your enquiry *re* "Tormentor for your fleas." May I ask, have you succeeded in getting at the meaning or origin of this curious street cry? I have tried to trace it, but in vain. It occurs to me as just possible that the following circumstance may bear on it :—

The Japanese are annoyed a good deal with fleas. They make little cages of bamboo—such I suppose as a small bird cage or mouse-trap—containing plenty of bars and perches inside. These bars they smear over with bird-lime, and then take the cage to bed with them. Is it not, as I say, *just possible*, that one

of

of our ancient mariners brought the idea home with him and started it in London? If so, a maker of bird cages or mouse-traps is likely to have put the idea into execution, and cried his mouse-traps and "flea tormentors" in one breath.

Faithfully yours,

DOUGLAS OWEN.

From "Notes and Queries," April 18th, 1885.

LONDON CRIES.—A cheap and extended edition of my *London Street Cries* being on the eve of publication, I shall be glad of early information as to the meaning of "A dip and a wallop for a bawbee"* and "Water for the buggs."* I recollect many years ago reading an explanation of the former, but am doubtful as to its correctness.

ANDREW W. TUER.

The Leadenhall Press, E.C.

One who was an Edinburgh student towards the end of last century told me that a man carrying a leg of mutton by the shank would traverse the streets crying "Twa dips and a wallop for a bawbee." This brought

---

* See p. 29.

the

the gude-wives to their doors with pails of boiling
water, which was in this manner converted into
"broth."

NORMAN CHEVERS, M.D.

32, Tavistock Road, W.
April 18*th*, 1885.

COCKNEY PRONUNCIATION.

25, ARGYLL ROAD, KENSINGTON, W.,
24*th April*, 1885.

DEAR MR. TUER,—

The Cockney sound of long *ā* which is confused
with received *ī*, is very different from it, and where it
approaches that sound, the long *ī* is very broad, so
that there is no possibility of confusing them in a
Cockney's ear. But is the sound Cockney? Granted
it is very prevalent in E. and N. London, yet it is
rarely found in W. and S.W. My belief is that it is
especially an Essex variety. There is no doubt about
its prevalence in Essex, so that [very roughly indeed]
"I say" there becomes "oy sy." Then as regards
the *ō* and *ou*. These are never pronounced alike.
The *ō* certainly often imitates received *ow*, though it
has more distinctly an *ō* commencement; but when
that

that is the case, *ou* has a totally different sound, which dialect-writers usually mark as *aow*, having a broad *ā* commencement, almost *a* in *bad*. Finer speakers— shopmen and clerks—will use a finer *a*. The sound of short *u* in *nut*, does not sound to me at all like *e* in *net*. There are great varieties of this " natural vowel," as some people call it, and our received *nut* is much finer than the general southern provincial and northern Scotch sounds, between which lie the mid and north England sounds rhyming to *foot* nearly, and various transitional forms. Certainly the sounds of *nut, gnat* are quite different, and are never confused by speakers ; yet you would write both as *net*.

The pronunciation of the Metropolitan area is ex- tremely mixed ; no one form prevails. We may put aside educated or received English as entirely arti- ficial. The N., N.E., and E. districts all partake of an East Anglian character ; but whether that is recent, or belongs to the Middle Anglian character of Mid- dlesex, is difficult to say. I was born in the N. district, within the sound of Bow Bells (the Cockney limits), over seventy years ago, and I do not recall the *ī.* pronunciation of *ā* in my boyish days, nor do I recollect having seen it used by the older humourists. Nor do I find it in " Errors of Pronunciation and Im- proper Expressions, Used Frequently and Chiefly by the
Inhabitants

Inhabitants of London," 1817, which likewise does not note any pronunciation of $\bar{o}$ like *ow*. Hence I am inclined to believe that both are modernisms, due to the growing of London into the adjacent provinces. They do not seem to me yet prevalent in the W. districts, though the N.W. is transitional. South of the Thames, in the S.W. districts, I think they are practically unknown. In the S.E. districts, which dip into N. Kent, the finer form of *aow* for *ou* is prevalent. The uneducated of course form a mode of speech among themselves. But I am sorry to find even school teachers much infected with the $\bar{\imath}$, *ow*, *aow*, pronunciations of $\bar{a}$, $\bar{o}$, *ou*, in N. districts.

Of course your Cockney orthography goes upon very broad lines, and you are quite justified in raising a laugh by apparent confusions, where no confusions are made by the speakers themselves, as Hans Breitmann did with the German. The confusion is only in our ears. They speak a language we do not use. To write the varieties of sounds, especially ot diphthongs, with anything like correctness, requires a phonetic alphabet which cannot even be read, much less written, without great study, such as you cannot look for in readers who want only to be amused. But another question arises, Should we lay down a pronunciation? There never has been any authority capable of doing
so

so. Orthoepists may protest, but the fashion of pronunciation will again change, as it has changed so
often and so markedly during the last six hundred
years ; see the proofs in my *Early English Pronunciation.* Why should we not pronounce *ā* as we do *ī*,
pronouncing *ī* as we do *oy*? Why should we not call
ō as we now call *ow*, pronouncing that as *aow*? Is not
our *ā* a change from *ī* (the German *ei*, *ai*) in *say*, *away*,
pain, etc.? Is not our *ou* a change from our sound of
oo in *cow*, etc.? Again, our *oo* replaces an old *oh* sound.
There is nothing but fashion which rules this. But
when sounds are changed in one set of vowels, a com-
pensating change takes places in another set, and so
no confusion results. In one part of Cheshire I met
with four sounds of *y* in *my*, never confused by natives,
although a received speaker hears only one, and all
arose from different sources. Why is one pronunciation *horrid* (or aw-ud), and another not? Simply
because they mark social grades. Of course I prefer
my own pronunciation, it's been my companion for so
many years. But others, just as much of course,
prefer theirs. When I brought out the *Phonetic News*,
in phonetic spelling, many years ago, a newsvendor
asked me, " Why write *neewz*? We always say *nooze*."

Very truly yours,

ALEXANDER J. ELLIS.

K

Index.

—

Size, large quarto : nearly out of print.

" The interest of the volume is inexhaustible."—*The Times.*

London Cries : With Six Charm-
ing Children printed direct from stippled plates
engraved in the Bartolozzi style.   The text by
ANDREW W. TUER, Author of " Bartolozzi and
his Works," &c.   LONDON : Field and Tuer,
The Leadenhall Press, E.C.

*One Guinea.   Large Paper Signed Proofs (250
   only) Two Guineas.   Large Paper Signed
   Proofs on Satin (50 only), Four Guineas.*

The twelve quaintly old fashioned and beautiful
whole-page illustrations are eminently adapted
for separate framing.

CONTAINS an account of London cries from the
   earliest period.   The " Six Charming Children "
—highly finished engravings of the Bartolozzi School
—are duplicated in red and brown.   There are in
addition about forty other illustrations—many of them
in colours—including ten of Rowlandson's humorous
subjects in facsimile, examples by George Cruikshank,
Joseph Crawhall, &c.

Tree Gossip. By Francis George

HEATH. LONDON: Field & Tuer, The Leadenhall Press. ⌊Three-and-Sixpence.

"Full of racy bits of gossip interspersed with valuable information, amusing anecdotes, and graceful descriptions." — *The Paper and Printing Trades Journal.*

Socialism of To-day. By Emile de

LAVELEYE. Translated from the French by GODDARD H. ORPEN. Including "Socialism in England," by the Translator. LONDON: Field & Tuer, The Leadenhall Press, E.C. [Six Shillings.

MR. ORPEN has largely added to the importance of this work by giving the first comprehensive account ever published of socialism in England.

Our Grandmothers' Gowns. By Mrs.

ALFRED W. HUNT. With Twenty-four hand-coloured Illustrations, drawn by G. R. HALKETT. LONDON: Field & Tuer. [Seven-and-Sixpence.

MRS. HUNT gives a short history of the dress of the period, in which she carefully preserves the original descriptions of the plates as given in contemporary fashion-books.

Tennis Cuts and Quips, in Prose and

VERSE, with Rules and Wrinkles. Edited by JULIAN MARSHALL, Author of "The Annals of Tennis," Hon. Sec. All England Lawn Tennis Club, Wimbledon. LONDON: Field & Tuer. [Two-and-Sixpence.

With *the latest* (1885) Alterations in Lawn Tennis Laws and Regulations.

The True Story of Mazeppa : The Son

OF PETER THE GREAT: A CHANGE OF REIGN. By
Viscount E. MELCHIOR DE VOGUE. Translated from the
French by JAMES MILLINGTON. LONDON : Field &
Tuer, The Leadenhall Press, E.C.   [Six Shillings.

THE weird story herein related possesses an equal interest
for the lover of the romantic and the historical.

Monsieur at Home.   By Albert Rhodes.

LONDON : Field & Tuer, The Leadenhall Press, E.C.
            [Two-and-Sixpence ; Cloth, Three-and-Sixpence.

"The typical Frenchman described by a shrewd and keen-witted
critic."

"A *very* good book indeed."—*Max O'Rell, Author of* "*John Bull
and his Island," "John Bull's Womankind," &c.*

Bartolozzi and his Works : Biographical,

Anecdotal, and Descriptive.   By ANDREW W. TUER.
LONDON : Field & Tuer, The Leadenhall Press, E.C.
                        [Twelve-and-Sixpence.

A COMPLETE guide to the study of old-fashioned prints.
Revised with new and interesting matter : in one thick
handsome vellum-bound volume, gold lettered, broad silken
bands and strings. *Limited to 500 signed and numbered copies.*

Life of Colonel Fred. Burnaby: By

R. K. MANN and J. REDDING WARE.   From MSS.
left by the Colonel just before he started for Egypt. Em-
bellished with a Portrait in Monochrome from the only
Photograph taken of Colonel Burnaby in recent years.
LONDON : Field & Tuer, The Leadenhall Press, E.C.
                        [Seven-and-Sixpence.

Izaak Walton : his Wallet Booke, being

the Songs in "THE COMPLEAT ANGLER" newly set forth and Illustrated by JOSEPH CRAWHALL. Hand-made paper; vellum bound, with inside humorously lettered silk-sewn pockets. *Edition-de-luxe*, limited and numbered. The numerous illustrations all separately hand-coloured. LONDON : Field & Tuer, The Leadenhall Press, E.C.
[One Guinea (500 Copies only) ; Large Paper, Two Guineas (100 copies only). Prices will be raised after publication.

ONE of Mr. Crawhall's engraved blocks—that is the boxwood block itself—will be attached as pendant to a silk bookmarker to *each copy of the large paper edition only.*

Songs of the North, gathered together

from the Highlands and Lowlands of Scotland. Edited by A. C. MACLEOD and HAROLD BOULTON. The Music arranged by MALCOLM LAWSON. LONDON : Field & Tuer, The Leadenhall Press, E.C. [One Guinea.

Why not eat Insects ? By Vincent M.

HOLT. LONDON : Field & Tuer, The Leadenhall Press, E.C. [One Shilling.

" THEM insects eats up every blessed green thing that do grow, and us farmers starves." "Well, eat *them* and grow fat !"

On the Stage — and Off : the Brief

Career of a Would-be Actor. By JEROME K. JEROME. LONDON : Field & Tuer, The Leadenhall Press.
[One Shilling.

Aspects of Fiction. By R. S. de C.

LAFFAN. LONDON : Field & Tuer, The Leadenhall
Press, E.C. [Half-a-Crown.

"Well written, sprightly, and eminently readable. Mr. Laffan's
arguments are logical and even brilliant."—*Notes and Queries.*

"A quaint specimen of the literature of a bygone age."

Old Aunt Elspa's A B C. Imagined

and Adorned by JOSEPH CRAWHALL. LONDON : Field
& Tuer.
[One Shilling, or Coloured throughout Two-and-Sixpence.

AN outrageously quaint book, full of illustrations.

"A volume to delight in."—*Pall Mall Gazette.*

Olde ffrendes wyth newe Faces: Adorn'd

with suitable Sculptures by JOSEPH CRAWHALL. *The
many hundreds of cuts being all hand-coloured, the issue is
necessarily limited.* LONDON : Field & Tuer, The
Leadenhall Press, E.C.
[In one thick 4to Volume, Twenty-five Shillings.

REPRODUCTIONS in facsimile of a large selection of the
crudely printed and humorously illustrated pamphlets that
were hawked about the country by the chapmen of a bygone
age. The illustrations will provoke smiles from the gravest.

Amateur Tommy Atkins: A Volunteer's

experiences related in the Letters of PRIVATE SAM^L BAG-
SHAW to his Mother. Illustrated with many clever silhou-
ettes. LONDON : Field & Tuer, The Leadenhall Press,
E.C. [One Shilling.

AN amusing relation of the experiences of a volunteer recruit
at drill, in camp, and on the march.